Pepe Escobar

2030

NIMBLE BOOKS LLC

NIMBLE BOOKS LLC

Nimble Books LLC
1521 Martha Avenue
Ann Arbor, MI, USA 48103
http://www.NimbleBooks.com
wfz@nimblebooks.com
+1.734-646-6277
Copyright 2015 by Pepe Escobar

Printed in the United States of America
ISBN-13: 978160880355

∞ The paper used in this publication meets the minimum requirements of the American National Standard for Information Sciences—Permanence of Paper for Printed Library Materials, ANSI Z39.48-1992. The paper is acid-free and lignin-free.

To Ayan, who will be 15 in 2030

NIMBLE BOOKS LLC

Oh, God said to Abraham, "Kill me a son"

Abe said, "Man, you must be puttin' me on"

God said, "No" Abe say, "What?"

God say, "You can do what you want, Abe, but

The next time you see me comin', you better run"

Well, Abe said, "Where d'you want this killin' done?"

God said, "Out on Highway 61"

Bob Dylan, Highway 61 Revisited

Five eleven twenty fifteen. The first moment I saw you. You were just a small constellation of thinly discernable lineaments pulsating on a scan. Light grey on black, vague silhouette, booming beat. Heart beat. Your Dad nailed it: "Sounds like techno." So you became The Little Techno Guy. What a party must have been in that amniotic liquid. Immobile. Under *that* rhythm. Swimming in liquid, plugged into deep bass headphones. Just a clinic in Barcelona, you inside your Mom's womb, and that primordial beat. So we just stayed there lost in reverie in the clinically aseptic room, swaying to your jungle beat.

Cut to a businessman swearing in Mandarin. I'm on a womb as well, aerial, one of my usual hangouts: the Asia-Europe shuttle, criss-crossing the sad dark night. I'm rewatching *The Big Sleep*. Bogie and Bacall, pagan celluloid divinities in black, white and shades of grey. *Life is in color but black and white is more realistic.* Sam Fuller. In *Pierrot Le Fou* by Godard, which will hit you in the stomach when you see it for the first time. But now Bacall asks Bogie, *You like to play games, don't you?* Oh no, this is hardly a game.

I have measured out my life not in coffee spoons— – that also applies— – but mostly in rock songs and airport lounges. Already in the 1980s we learned that in the future they would be all indistinguishable —airport lounges, shopping malls, hospitals, prisons. And I have measured out my life in silences. Deep into the night. White nights.

Enjoy the silence. Wish I could, like you do now.

Never thought I'd last this long. You will see that I'm just another conglomeration of cells issued from the "Die young, stay pretty, leave a beautiful corpse" generation, which instead persisted, against a few odds, to go deeper into the sound of fury, signifying nothing, knowing full well *the wreck of body, slow decay of blood, testy delirium, or dull decrepitude, or what worse evil come* would one day reap its reward. *Got to meet our death one day.* Blind Willie McTell. The blues will never lie to you.

Somehow, the Grim Reaper's usual policies seem to have been loosened up in my case. It might have been on acid – a bad one-way trip to the other side. It might have been that al-Qaeda missile which missed my van on the way to Jalalabad by a split second. It might have been arriving fifteen seconds too early to a car bombing in al-Saddoon street in Baghdad. Or the heart— – not of darkness—might have simply decided to quit the game. Instead, fate has blessed me to be on my way to finally see you being born.

So I drink in your honor many a memory and desire Martini – celebrating what will be forged in your soul, that wacky concept we call the life of Man—*solitary, poor, nasty, brutish and short.* Carrying all the inbuilt requisite redeeming qualities, such as the smile of the woman you love, a bottle of Margaux, Platonic banquets with dear friends, the perfect sunset in Brittany? New Mexico? Patagonia? Bali?... and the sound of silence. So, *before I slip... into the Big Sleep/ I want to hear... I want to hear... the scream of the butterfly.* The butterfly tells me here and now is 2030 and you are opening this letter. I may be long gone. So from aerial womb to aquatic womb, here's to life, love and the pursuit of ...

Life. Shakespeare will tell you. A sorry tale. Told by an idiot. Full of sound and fury. Signifying nothing. But what about those wild strawberries? That's from another movie. Bergman. What we take away, in the end, are the wild strawberries.

So here's a tale told by an idiot signifying—maybe—something. The White Queen in *Alice in Wonderland* swears she can believe "six impossible things before breakfast." I couldn't possibly require you to be a believer —in anything. But let me try to unveil to you a basket of lateral? parallel? underground? desires. To arouse your sense of Beauty—and Wonder. To take you behind the red curtains that protect The Forest. To suggest you a few keys for reading The Book.

Your Dad, diver extraordinaire, will teach you everything about Nature—and the sea. He *could have been a pair of ragged claws, scuttling across the floors of silent seas.* Yes, he lived it all, as you will learn, from Zanzibar to Sulawesi. Wild horses? He's the man. Serengeti lions? He's the man. He will show you some of the Greatest Hits Nature has accomplished after four and a half billion years of R&D.

Nature's got style. Gorgeous style. You may conceive the world as a piece of art, produced in a quite distinctive style. We could even see it as an apotheosis of symmetry. Ancient Greece already dabbled with the—modern—idea that nature uses symmetry to construct the world.

The idea has been used in physics and mathematics as what funky scientists call a very Buddhist "change without change." From symmetry as "change without change," you get to the laws of physics—or at least the equations that express them. The theory of relativity taught us that if we view the world from a moving train—or an aerial womb—things may look different, but the same laws of physics apply. So take a look at those perfect equations whose consequences remain unchanged, even under myriad transformations. These are the circles among the equations. They actually run the world.

Art and science hit the same layers of the brain. And our little brain has developed a real kick: to reward us for interacting with Beauty. *A thing of beauty is a joy forever.* Keats. When in doubt, grab that Keats. The *Collected Poems*, in my *bibliothèque*, which—first revelation!—is bound to become your *bibliothèque*. No, you won't get a trust fund or a Maserati GranTurismo Stradale (but you will get a cool black Alfa Romeo). You will get books.

You will see that throughout history, for an array of different societies, writing and the Word have incarnated magic—secret sacred arts. From the beginning, to write and to name are sortileges through which the spirit incarnates nature. Writing was deemed to be a gift from the gods. Only The Priest could practice it. If a young man decided to become initiated, that was a miracle. So writing was a hermetically closed domain, under protection of the gods. Imagine becoming aware of the secrets of writing amidst hordes of illiterates dwelling in extremely hierarchical cultures. That was pure magic. Black—and white—magic.

The art of reading is a branch of the art of living. I could not possibly wish you to be drowned in an ocean of books, but to find the way to surf the waves by what you would be able to live in books. If life is not the antithesis of spirit—and that is still a major "if"—we can always rely on some Masters and how they have evolved throughout their lives. Like a character in a Borges short story—Borges! That virtually blind South American Buddha in a grey suit—I would love you to become a pilgrim for eons in the countless rooms of their temple, exploring labyrinths, caverns, oceans. *Everything, in the world, exists to end up in a book.* Mallarmé. Borges went further—it's more like we are all the verses or the letters of a magical book. *This incessant book is the only thing that exists in the world. It is the world.*

By now you may have read *Siddhartha* by Herman Hesse—I did it when I was your age. He wrote extensively about an ideal *bibliothèque*. Not as infinite as Borges imagined the *Biblioteca de Babel*. *The universe (which others name La Biblioteca) … Like all men of the Biblioteca, I traveled in my youth—pilgrimages in search of a book and maybe the catalogue of catalogues.* The narrator affirms that the Biblioteca is interminable. Unlimited. But also periodical. If there were an eternal traveler to traverse it, centuries would make him learn that *the same volumes always repeat themselves in the same disorder—which, repeated, turn into an order: the Order.* Borges called it "an elegant hope." When I visited Borges with a dear friend at his apartment in Buenos Aires, for one of his last interviews before his twilight—he recited Blake and Icelandic sagas to us while drifting into a literary trance across his sofa—we noticed that the beloved treasures in the living room *bibliothèque* were not about quantity. The Order was all about editing.

So taking a cue from Hesse—and Borges—this may be the basic scheme of your ideal *bibliothèque*, which you may find in my, your own *bibliothèque*. Borges also imagined a Platonic work, hereditary, transmitted from father to son, with each new individual adding a chapter or carefully correcting the page of his heirs. So here's your hereditary *bibliothèque*. Feel free to recite it as a mantra.

The Upanishads. The Buddha sermons—and you will find some fabulous translations from Sanskrit to English I brought from Calcutta. The *Gilgamesh*—the Babylonian epic. The *Analects* of Confucius. The *Tao* by Lao Tzu, and the writings of Chiang Tzu. Classical Chinese poems. It's practically all there—the cult of natural forces through divine figures, side by side with the feeling that gods are symbols. And the notion that joy and suffering in life are to a great extent dependent on Man's actions.

You will be ready to let Scheherazade guide you through *The Thousand and One Nights*. Persia: a collection of Hafez and Omar Khayyam. Aeschylus, Sophocles and Euripides. Plutarch. Lucian. Horace, Virgil, Ovid, Tacitus—and Suetonius. And Petronius's *Satyricon* written under Nero. Dante's *Divine Comedy*. Boccacio's *Decameron*. The poems of Michelangelo. The *Lives* of Renaissance geniuses by Vasari. The autobiography of Cellini.

King Arthur and the Knights of the Round Table. The *Tristan* from Gottfried von Strassburg. The *Parsifal* from Wolfram. The poems of Villon. The *Gargantua and Pantagruel* from Rabelais. The *Fables* of La Fontaine. The theatre of Molière. The *Candide* from Voltaire. The *Confessions* of Rousseau. The *Essays* of Montaigne. Virtually all Stendhal—especially *Le Rouge et le Noir* and *La Chartreuse de Parme*. The

Flowers of Evil by Baudelaire. Much Balzac, but mostly as much Flaubert as possible—from *L'Education Sentimentale* to *Madame Bovary*. Verlaine poems, and most of all, Rimbaud, from *Bateu Ivre* to *Une Saison en Enfer*.

Chaucer's *Canterbury Tales*. Milton's *Paradise Lost*. All Swift. *Robinson Crusoe* and *Moll Flanders* by Defoe. Fielding's *Tom Jones*. *Tristram Shandy* by Sterne. All Keats. All Shelley. Byron's *Childe Harold*. De Quincey's *Confession of an English Opium Eater*. Carlyle's *Sartor Resartus*. Thackeray's *Vanity Fair*. So much Dickens. Poems of Swinburne. Oscar Wilde's *Dorian Gray*. All Poe. Much Whitman.

Don Quixote. Icelandic sagas—like *Skalden Egil*. Andersen's tales. Most Ibsen. Gogol's *Dead Souls*. Gontcharov's *Oblomov*. Turgenev's *Father and Son*. Tolstoy's *Anna Karenina* and *War and Peace*. As much Dostoyevsky as possible—start with *Crime and Punishment*, delve into *The Devils* and reach the apotheosis with the Karamazovs.

Goethe, from *Werther* to *Faust*. Historical and aesthetic texts by Schiller. A Holderlin Greatest Hits. Selected Novalis. All Kleist. The *Elixirs of the Devil* by E.T.A. Hoffmann. Heine's prose. And fragment upon fragment of badass Nietzsche.

And then you will find the elective affinities, the *coups de coeur*—a whole universe unto themselves, those that grab you by the soul and grow on you as the years go by. Bataille. Lautréamont. Kafka. Sade. Céline. Camus. Georg Trakl. Lévi-Strauss. James Frazer's *The Golden Bough*. Schopenhauer. Fitzgerald. Hemingway. Ginsberg. Auden.

Cioran. Michaux. Villiers de L'Isle. Schwob. Karl Kraus. Musil. Roberto Arlt. All Conrad. And the magic quartet: Yeats, Eliot, Pound and Joyce.

Waalll, by the time you've read them all you will be a *seeerious karakter*—as Pound would call it. And you'd have been initiated in the whole family folklore about how, after taking your Grandma carrying your Dad in her belly on a mini-Grand Tour of Italy—she was *La Rotonda*, after Palladio—I escaped to Dublin to literally walk the eighteen chapters of Joyce's *Ulysses*, kept going across the then Iron Curtain, and was hurled back to drive Grandma on a rickety Kombi—owned by star photographer Great Grandma—to the hospital singing *Satisfaction* by the Stones just in time for your Dad to be born. But that's another *riverrun*.

In Dublin, retracing *Ulysses*, I could really feel how the soul of one man can represent all men, how the soul of Dedalus was representing the soul of my still unborn son. Or as Joyce told it in *Finnegans Wake, the soul of everyelsebody rolled into olesoleself.*

And then, while navigating the *bibliothèque*, you will find that verse from Baudelaire in the epigraph of Conrad's *The Shadow Line*. The sea—as much as being the mirror of fiction—is a boundless space for the projection of human affection. So here's to literature as *water, water everywhere,* as in Coleridge's *Ancient Mariner*; as life; and as a music of the spheres.

Equations describing musical instruments are equivalent to equations establishing how atoms work. Things that vibrate in atoms are of course more abstract than a piano; they dance with the colors of light that a particular atom loves to emit—or absorb. And here is our first great intuition by the Ancient Greeks; Pythagoras associated the movement of the planets with the music of the spheres. So back to Nature, and what atoms are all about; musical instruments unveiling the perfect music of the spheres.

Like the jazz of Monk and Coltrane. Dissident and melodic—simultaneously.

玄奘

What is the life force of civilization? Genius. There is even a formula for genius linking to genius across history—*each giant calling to his brother through the desolate intervals of time.* Who said that? An English Romantic like Shelly? No: a Buddhist-influenced German philosopher, and Nietzsche's intellectual model: Schopenhauer.

There would have been so many—infinite—stories to tell you. Why these—now? Why not? Yes, it's all about editing. And not going on and on and on, like Scheherazade. *Riverrun.* Watch the river flow.

So here's our first story. If I had to compact a short history of "our" world, what we call Western Civilization, of which you are about to become a member, born in Barcelona, which is Catalunya, and which is not Spain, a citizen of the European Union—that idea oh so midwifed by American elites and now oh so mired in existential crisis—our story would have to start at the Greek bazaar.

What a party! Epicureans, Stoics, Cynics, Skeptics. Epicurus: in the end we're nothing but a bunch of atoms, musical instruments unveiling the—imperfect?—music of the spheres. We pass randomly though life, and that's it. Death is oblivion—right where we started in the first place. *In the end is my beginning.* What's left is to live for the moment.

I suspect you will be exhilarated at how Epicurus issued no less than a declaration of war against the superpowers of the time; against the Lyceum of Aristotle—the universe is not immortal and endless!—and against the Academy of Plato—out with reason, all for hedonism. No wonder Socrates and Plato recoiled in horror.

So essentially we got a God that could not give a damn. An empty sky—from where no fabulously fleshy Tintoretto-depicted angels are falling from. A random—meaningless—world below. What we got was Shakespeare, centuries before the bard, a racket full of sound and fury, signifying nothing.

Then there was this fellow Antisthenes, the poor son of an Athenian and a Thracian slave, who renounced all material possessions to teach at a gym—the Cynosarges, a big hit with the proletariat in Athens. But the real deal was his disciple Diogenes, through whom Cynicism was key to shape the Greek and Roman vision of the world.

Diogenes, the first homeless philosopher (with no access to a soup kitchen, and no unemployment benefits) was convinced we need to own absolutely nothing to be truly free. You will know that he lived inside a huge jar outside a temple in Athens and begged for food in the street. Talk about fabulous PR skills. A superstar. Can't beat walking the streets of Athens with a lantern looking for an honest man (he didn't find any). Or begging for food from a statue; "I'm learning to deal with rejection."

Diogenes wanted his lantern to shine like a laser on the faces of all the people—and institutions—protected inside Plato's cozy cave, where we mistake the reflections projected on the walls for "reality." Alexander the Great famously said that were he not Alexander, he would want to be Diogenes. But we don't know if Diogenes would ever want to be Alexander.

I bet Alexander would have loved to be Italian. Italy civilized the world not only once but twice. You will have plenty of time to mull about it over many a Platonic banquet featuring the perfect *papardelle al cinghiale* and the perfect bottle of Brunello. For the Roman Empire chapter, you will find all you need in the *bibliothèque*, from Tacitus to Gibbon. For the Renaissance chapter you may want to know a few crucial things that happened before.

Do you know what Turkish Sultan Mehmet did when he conquered Constantinople in 1453, in front of the Church of Holy Wisdom? We learned from Gibbon that he sang a Persian song, softly, almost whispering: *The spider has woven his web in the imperial pal-*

ace, and the owl has sung her watch-song on the towers of Afrasiab.
Persia. How chic is that? Well, Persia was way more civilized than
Greece—but that, again, is another story.

What we're focusing on now is an epic Hollywood never dared to
tackle. Constantinople, the capital of the Byzantine Roman Empire—
Rum to the Arabs and Turks—had fallen. That was Europe's last ten-
uous link to the glorious age of the Caesars in Rome. It became Muslim and now was named Istanbul. The greatest church in the world
would be turned into a mosque.

Our camera though prefers to slide out of a panoramic shot and
focus on Greek refugees—actually scholars—escaping in droves carrying loads of ... books. The preferred safe haven was Italy. Soon we
had stacks of manuscripts filling the library of the monastery of San
Marco in Florence. Cosimo de Medici was the monastery's benefac-
tor. Among the manuscripts were the lost dialogues of Plato. And
that's how Plato—not lost in translation—became the driver of the
apex of European civilization.

One fine day Cosimo said to Marsilio Ficino, the six-year-old son
of his doctor: "Someday you will grow up to translate those works
and reveal their secrets to the world."

And that's exactly what the boy did. Marsilio founded the Platonic
Academy in Florence, promoting Plato's idea of freedom through the
creative spirit. The Renaissance was a very big deal: no less than the
birth of the modern world. Imagine Plato rejoicing in some heavenly

sphere. Plato's books—apart from the *Timaeus*—had been "lost" for almost five centuries. But during the 1100s, Arab libraries carefully protected Platonic dialogues—which were later "adopted" by Latin translators. How could we ever thank those Greek scholars "invading" Italy in the 1400s—before and after the fall of Constantinople?

Take all the time in the world to wade through Plato's *Symposium*—or how to kick philosophic ass at a wine party. The Platonic banquet may well be the emblem of what's best about our little lives—the meeting of beauty and intellect, thesis and pleasure.

The theme of the Platonic banquet was to praise the goddess of Love in all manner of sensuality overtones. When Socrates starts talking, it's all about "Love is Desire Aroused by Beauty." Ultimate love goes way beyond carnal desire, aspiring to a spiritual truth. And physical beauty stars as a direct material copy of the ineffable, as much as material objects are copies of Platonic forms.

Socrates tells us that the true spiritual nature of love was revealed to him by—who else—a woman, the priestess Diotima. So our love of beauty leads to a love of truth. Keats once again: *Beauty is truth, and truth is beauty.* But Socrates also said that our love of beauty leads to the Walhalla: God. "A sight of divine beauty itself"—which is the highest kind of knowledge, and love. Because, after all, our soul shares the same divine nature.

And that's how a sexy stripper can lead us to God. Well, not really. Which brings us to the Botticelli babes.

I wish I could take you there. In my post-college days in Florence, in the late 1970s, a British girlfriend got me a job as a guide for Oxford and Cambridge graduates on their Grand Tour of European civilization. To get their attention I would compare Botticelli with David Bowie—and I was in business. *Starman, waiting in the sky …*

Spring and *The Birth of Venus* were the Top of the Pops at the time. After all they were inspired by love ballads, written by Poliziano, a disciple of Ficino. They evoke "girls in a ring"—not bikini wrestlers, that would be the American pop version—but The Three Graces, a pagan mythology allegory. Ficino described The Three Graces as symbols of the circular—Nietzsche does Florence?—movement of divine love, from God to soul and back to heaven again. There was also the motif of the triad—a Pythagorean symbol of wholeness, perfection. And the Graces were of course connected with the pagan goddess of Love, Venus. Superstar Venus makes a flashy appearance not once but twice—splendorous in delicate drapery and then nude as she emerges, just born in full form, from the sea.

The birth of Venus is in itself a triad. On the left of the painting you will see "passionate winds" depicting the tumult of Eros, the carnal power of love. On the right is the allegory of Spring, with her delicate clothes on, offering a cloak to the nude Venus. Physical—profane—love is transformed into chaste divine love, the apex of Platonism. It's not by accident that the gorgeous face of Venus would

NIMBLE BOOKS LLC

end up dissolving into Botticelli's myriad paintings of the Virgin Mary.

In the *Timaeus*, according to Ficino, Plato places Love at the heart of the primeval Chaos from which cosmic order is born. So that's another version of the Big Bang for you; Love exploding everywhere. The Birth of Venus as fusion of body and soul—unity of the cosmos. Buddhist Venus?

From the Botticelli room at the Uffizi, in the ideal Grand Tour of our own triad—you, your Dad and me—we would transfer, by Alfa Romeo, from Florence to Rome all the way to the Stanza della Segnatura, the Raphael rooms at the Vatican. And then an awesome Greek philosophy spectacular will be unveiled—Raphael's *School of Athens*, inspired by another genius, Pico della Mirandola, a seriously good looking man who scholars loved to describe as "the last man to know everything."

So in the *School of Athens* we have Pico beside Plato standing next to Pythagoras. The whole gang is there: Euclid, Diogenes, Epicurus, Socrates. And Plato and Aristotle as princes of philosophy—Plato holding a copy of the *Timeaus*, Aristotle a copy of the *Nicomachean Ethics*. The architectural setting could not but be a triad—three barrel vaults, a Trinity, as the interpenetration of Plato and Aristotle, as Pico saw it, prefigures the unity of God.

This is oh so Platonist—as The Big Picture is what really matters. You will soon discover how the small fragments—opposites clashing—fit together into a wondrous coherent whole.

Florence. One of the key decisions of my life was to live in Florence to learn about the Apex of Art on the spot. My Virgil was of course Dante's *Divina Commedia*. A small room in via Faenza. A favorite trattoria. A few selected books. Hours and hours spent in silent contemplation. And bicycling to the countryside to check out that fresco or that glazed terracotta roundel. It was also easy to picture why Donatello and Brunelleschi went to Rome to study classical sculpture and architecture. Classical architecture had been preserved in Italian city life since the fall of the Roman Empire. As much as political freedom had been preserved by Cicero—which scholars in Italy had been reading since the 1100s.

Donatello and Brunelleschi came back—and what civilization got in return includes the androgynous David now at the Bargello and the Duomo in Florence. Creativity does not even begin to describe three blessed generations of Florentines. Why Florence, you would ask? Vasari, who knew most of the superstars, said Florence's political freedom inspired critical thinking—*the air of Florence making minds naturally free, and not content with mediocrity.* And of course a lot of hard study was involved. *Studia humanitatis*—the study of humanity. For Renaissance humanists this amounted to plunging into history (essentially Ancient Greece and Rome); rhetoric (following the example of Cicero); Greek and Roman literature; and moral philosophy (basically Aristotle's *Ethics*). Call it the tools of freedom.

How I wish the family triad could one day discuss all this over perfect bottles of Brunello at my favorite joint near the Pitti Palace, setting the stage for a perfect Platonic banquet. Those wild strawberry moments.

I'll be skipping the Enlightenment and even the French eighteenth century—scorching elegance distilled in epithets—to cut to the chase and introduce you to Nietzsche, in fact circling back all the way to his, my beloved pre-Socratics. Thales, Anaximander, Anaxagoras, Parmenides, Democritus and Nietzsche's favorite, Heraclitus. Imagine that what they wrote, after 2500 years, had virtually vanished. Only fragments remained, quoted by Plato and Aristotle, but manipulated to deride the pre-Socratics.

Enter Nietzsche the guerilla: both Plato and Aristotle got it wrong. The real badasses were the pre-Socratics. Heraclitus taught us that "all things change"—no less than Buddhist impermanence. He denied Being. Impermanence should eventually lead us to serenity. So we should deal with ceaseless change. Ride the hurricane.

Ride the hurricane. Byronic Romanticism remixing primordial Greek philosophy. With Dionysus as the driving force of creative insight, prevailing over Apollo as the symbol of cold hard reason. Baddass Nietzsche hailed the free, spontaneous spirit of Dionysus— and the pre-Socratics—inspiring music, art, poetry, drama but on many occasions crushed by the cold, calculating reason of Plato and Apollonian man.

There are few things in life that will hit you in the guts with such power such as Nietzsche telling the story of the West going downhill. The screenplay includes of course a sequence in the suburbs of the Roman Empire as an obscure Jewish sect—Christianity—turned Plato into the ethical framework of a whole society. For Nietzsche, Christianity is "Platonism for the masses." Of course we could mightily disagree when he asserted that freedom only prevailed briefly during the Renaissance, before the Enlightenment and the modern age were trapped inside Plato's reason. But he's got a point.

And that brings us to will to power. The Homeric heroes, the pre-Socratics, had it. The barbaric "blonde beasts" who destroyed the Roman Empire, had it. Genghis Khan had it. Tamerlane had it. For Hegel and for Nietzsche, historical progress shows off drenched in blood. It's as if they were already justifying the next World War—out of which we will all … vanish?

God, at least, was dead at the end of the nineteenth century. Dostoyevsky laid down the law: "if God is dead, everything is permitted." Nietzsche amplified it; "What does not destroy us makes us stronger." Death of Socrates, death of God. What's left? We must become Dionysus free spirits. We will plunge into a world beyond good and evil. And we will be back to the point where Heraclitus began. *In the end is my beginning.*

By this stage you might be suspecting that Epicurus, Democritus, Lucretius, and good ol' Uncle Marx, were all invested in the absolute opposite of the notion that dominated the West culturally for centuries, derived from—who else—Plato, and then Christian Neoplatonism, for whom reality is not what we see and sense, but the Idea.

So up there in the heavens there is nothing apart from astral bodies. No supra-sensible powers. No theological fantasies. No Gods. No God.

Thus Nature is nothing but space and time; time of stars, of seasonal cycles, of germination, fecundation, labor, the labor of time. Thus this Nietzsche power cocktail of living life as a sort of Solar Eroticism. To empty heaven and earth from every obscure, or institutionally religious, force. And to celebrate hedonism, atheism and even post-anarchism as life forces. And here's another—possible—revelation. This might be one of the possible—unconscious?—reasons your parents Named you (remember, the sacred power of the Word) Ayan. Way towards the Sun.

玄奘

"Reality" may be no more than a warped painting with figures speaking in unknown code. And then, one day, in the jingle jangle morning you'll come following a Mr. Tambourine Man.

Turn on. Tune in. No need to drop out. Go with the flow. And relish the powerful visionary fragrance. You will be 15, but you will be transported to when you're 24, as Bob Dylan was at the time, illuminated by a fertile, intriguing, erudite fantasy. That was 50 years before now—when you're about to be born. Just like your Dad's hymn, for quite a while, was Hendrix's *Purple Haze*—he must have listened to it for the first time when he was only a few weeks old, in one of our morning pram-pushing walks in the park, the Walkman blasting in his head—yours may be *Mr. Tambourine Man* by The Byrds, or Dylan meets the Beatles.

And then one day, when you're already immersed in the fight against your demons, you will definitely feel *Like a Rolling Stone*—a cut-up evoking Burroughs, Ginsberg and Kerouac born as a 20-page vomit, hate and vendetta turned into an over six-minute single. And then we will revisit Highway 61 all the way—those 2,264 kilometers from New Orleans via Memphis to the depths of Minnesota. We will stop at the crossroads—well, not the real crossroads—where Robert Johnson sold his soul to the devil. And the blues will guide you towards the sun.

Very soon in life you will have had the intuition that music hits you like a running blaze on a plain. A flash of lightning crisscrossing the clouds. Conrad will tell you that we live as we dream, alone. Addendum: we live in the flicker. One flicker after another. *Only a flicker/over the strained time-ridden faces/distracted from distraction by distraction.*

In Plato's dialogues you will see how harmony derives from the construction of the solar system. It's not impossible for us to eventually perceive—in a flicker—the inner workings of our cosmic resonance chamber.

My generation happened to be growing up when pop music defied every cultural and political limit, even ideology. Music was central to everything. Back to The Byrds. On *5D*, out in 1966—that's when psychedelia irrupted into mass culture—they were already venturing about thinking in five dimensions, already previewing that our little world is just a finite planet which can be seen from outside in an infinite universe. And the music told the story.

Eight Miles High meant we could just leave our contained life on Earth and fly away from everything we knew, looking down, oh so benign, way from above. *Mr. Spaceman* is about visionaries from other planets. Bowie a few years later would confess *planet earth is blue and there's nothing I can do*. But we thought we could.

And then we had the ultimate structural connection between the trip to outer space and the journey into our inner space; the final sequence in Kubrick's *2001: A Space Odyssey*. I only really got the picture when I saw it on acid.

My generation was largely shaped by Vietnam—what the Vietnamese called, and I learned on the spot, years later, The American War; that furious amalgamation of free-fire zones, assassinations, torture, napalm and agent orange incineration rituals, the staggering body count convulsing a small, distant peasant land which we, the young, admired as the cradle of heroic guerrillas. So how could we not be shaped by Nick Ut's 1972 shot of a young Vietnamese girl napalmed by a South Vietnamese plane running naked in pain and terror.

I was only 14 in 1968. I could not possibly cover Vietnam as a journalist. So I watched it from afar, listening to Doors and Hendrix and Stax and Motown—and would only finally "see" it on Coppola's Heart of Darkness-based *Apocalypse Now*. That's all you need to know, your crash course on war—and the folly of war.

What I mostly lived on This Side of Paradise was the California dream. Flower power, soft Hinduism, Buddhist chic, paisley Nietzsche and Schopenhauer—groovin' to Cream and The Who, Beach Boys and Deep Purple, Sly and the family Stone and Booker T. and the MGs, all peppered with a healthy dose of Frank Zappa freakout cynicism. We had our own, private *folie à quatre*—two guys, two beautiful girls—blossoming in a multicolored bubble under an ironclad military dictatorship way down in South America. Smashing, baby!

And that's when I started the long, long trip—through the looking glass—to break on through to the other side: Asia.

Non-Western thought was not invented in California, of course, not even by Ginsberg and the beats, the predecessors of the Bay Area hippies. But that was the entrance ticket for so many of us to Hinduism and Buddhism—and to Asia. Well, California was, is, always, a flashy, glitzy preview of worlds to come.

So when you see a catalogue of an exhibition in Berlin in the 2010s about California in the *bibliothèque* you might be able to experiment it all, in words, and a few images, in retrospect, like your portable *2001: A Space Odyssey*. By then you will have listened to playlist after playlist crafted by your Dad and me—a limitless soundtrack, an uninterrupted "Ode to Joy." How I wish you could have inherited it all—grooves as precious as the finest jade; a vinyl collection. But that was implacably decimated over years of nomadism. A nomad may carry his favorite carpet—the Silk Qom, straight out of his original home at the Aleppo bazaar, which you will meet as dot com. Or the prayer carpet from the bazaar in Herat (others were, what else, consumed by flames in a ceremonial fire in Thailand). But a nomad cannot carry stacks of vinyl (although I did, for years, between continents). You may still find the first American pressing of *Band of Gypsies* and the first British pressing of *Quadrophenia*. All else had been stolen. Disappeared from a container. Never returned. Buddhist impermanence. But you will get it all—bootlegs, outtakes included—on digital.

So, plugged to the uninterrupted "Ode to Joy," you will see how the battlefield was arranged. Picture an ominous technological determinism versus Back to Nature Romanticism—or, to spice it up with fragrant romance, the hippie revolt. The reason why this was, and remains, so absolutely crucial is that the rise of computer culture in the San Francisco Bay Area came out of this mix. The California cosmology. Digital network capitalism would then shape post-modern globalization, from the New Economy before the end of the millennium to every digital wall to be broken beyond. California cosmology forged our world. The world you're about to be born into.

It was all played out in 1968. Not the end of colonial capitalist modernity—not even remotely. Rather the blueprint, the whole set of conditions, for the rise of a more solid—or *all that's solid melts into air*—follow-up. Way, way beyond mere co-opting or assimilating the dissidence of counterculture.

I had run conceptual rings around this for so many years, in my flower power days, in college, at the Free University in Amsterdam in the late 1970s, when I lived in Hollywood, in my nomadic East-West shuttle, but then I had this—Benjamin-inspired—aesthetic illumination in Berlin, a quarter of a century after the reunification of Germany. For so long I thought that 1968 was defined by May 68 in France. *It's forbidden to forbid. Be realist, demand the impossible.* No. 1968 was actually defined by the picture of planet Earth—it's blue, and there's nothing I can do—transmitted by Apollo 8.

Since the end of the Second World War—which your Great Grand Dad fought—modernity expanded like a hurricane. At the same time the powers that be consented to a redeployment of what was originally excluded and derided as The Other: everything that was considered irrational, affective, playful—and foreign. Exclusion was the essential precondition for non-stop expansion of the exploitation of the colonized, as in the majority of the people on Earth.

And guess where, geographically, this new conception of history was forged: California. That's where Western colonial expansion reached the limit—no chance of being submerged in the Pacific!—and then changed direction: from outward expansion to ... inner turmoil.

I come from the second tranche of the baby boomer big bang. Those of us born between 1946 and 1957 did get the best music, the best sex, the best chances to "make it." Life is an unfair affair; born too late to be killed in Vietnam—even as a journalist—and too early to be smashed and gobbled up alive by the Age of Austerity.

So picture the end of the 1960s and throughout the 1970s as a roving axis between psychedelia and computer culture, trespassed by hippies, cyberneticians, Back to Nature Romantics, techno worshippers, disco transsexuals—and a lot of freaks. Everybody shared a deep rejection of hierarchy and authoritarian power structures—what we called "the system." Utopia was to explore all sorts of outlaw space, in what those visionary Frenchmen, Deleuze and Guattari, which I had the honor to meet much later would define as a rhizomatic way, war machines deployed like rats prowling in the underground.

It couldn't get more romantic than that: our categorical imperative was to fight Them. With their vision of planetary totality enshrined in a formula called Cold War. Forget about any notion of "peace." Instead we had a Monster—listen to the song, by Steppenwolf—overrunning the planet and threatening life and nature with nuclear bombs. You will become familiar with the acronym MAD (Mutually Assured Destruction). "The system" was not about the liberating power of the cyberworld but a sinister opaque oligarchic raw power enshrined in the industrial-military complex.

We had no guns but we had The Doors. That's in that playlist, probably the first I had ever thought to plug between your ears, with all the studio outtakes and the best of the best live shows. *The End*—the end of the Californian desert, the end of the Western frontier, the end of all elaborate plans of Western dominance. And then the music's over—*the earth is ravaged and plundered and raped her and bit her/ stuck her with knives in the side of the dawn/ and tied her with fences and dragged her down.* And then The Lizard King launches into what would turn into the star 1968 graffiti in the walls of the Quartier Latin: *We want the world and we want it now.*

So rivers of acid and tax-free import of Spiritual Asia led to cybernetics as a neo-animist principle. That was The Great Reconnection, the end of alienation—but running in parallel to the naturalization and humanization of capitalism. Objective reality became totally dissolved in information flows and "relationships." Baudrillard would later bundle it all up as simulacra. We talked about it, laughing, at a party in Rio while he couldn't take his eyes away from the non-stop fabulous parade of gorgeous nymphs.

And all that ended up coalescing as Google and Facebook posing as The World. Space all around us was romanticized as space of unlimited freedom and spontaneous harmony—but with no inbuilt demand for political transformation. What we all inherited was the California Transformer Cosmology. Liberating ideas transformed into the liberation of markets and the liberalization of capitalist economy, yielding a ready-made escapist ideology perfect for … slaves?

You're about to be born into the ceaseless digital proliferation of *everything*. Borges: the map has not become equal to the world, but exceeds the world. And the map simply won't go away: on the contrary, like Baudrillard had already intuited, it's reality that's disintegrating. For Baudrillard, the "positive absorption into the transparency of the computer" is even worse than alienation. We are all absorbed by the looking glass. Only a few may eventually get though. The 21st century remix of the *Discourse on Voluntary Servitude* by Étienne de la Boétie still needs to come out.

So, all those years ago, it's as if we were living in some sort of Arcadia. My generation was granted so many privileged stops along the way—starting with that ease, and simplicity, and fun back in the 1970s that no longer exists. Education was not an abhorrent treadmill in which a degree only mattered as a passport to the job market. Jobs would just pop up. Social mobility was a fact of life. Class was a cultural construct, not economic at all. We could always get a break. I could abandon college and go on a long Scandinavia summer trek in

1975 and then go back to college. I could decide not to do a PhD and instead live in a bedsit in London in 1977 and 1978 hitting every gig in town from The Clash and The Jam to Blondie and Television. Many of us ripped through the Last Days of the Cold War go-go 1980s—from New York, L.A. and Sao Paulo to London, Paris and Tokyo, bending every hedonist barrier.

Yet what is your generation inheriting? Jobs that do not even qualify as insecure. Totally de-unionized workplaces—as in every boy and girl for—savage social Darwinist—him/herself. "Internships" that qualify as slave labor at best. Exploding transportation costs. The proverbial sky-high rents and property prices in Europe's major cities. Creaking beyond belief public services. And essentially a *polis* that has lost, or has been deprived, of any sense of community and collective spirit.

So the generation who took social mobility for granted and enjoyed a We're In It Together ethos ended up carving an abyss, making it practically impossible for the less privileged among the generations that followed to break through—to the pleasant side.

Talking bout my generation. *Hope I die before I get old.* Many of us—mentally, ethically—did.

玄奘

Let me tell you another story. It was the summer of 2000. I was crossing Afghanistan, actually Talibanistan, from east to west with my dear friend, ace photographer Jason. We were in the middle of

NIMBLE BOOKS LLC

the burning hot desert, somewhere in Helmand province, which the Americans, years later, would try to tame, of course unsuccessfully. Desert, desert everywhere, and all we had on board were a few bottles of warm Pepsi. We also needed gas, badly. Then, in the distance, not a mirage, we saw a gas station; actually a squalid shack manned by a kid with a few plastic bottles of Pepsi filled with gasoline. He started filling our tank—with his gaze locked on me. Who was that foreign devil? What was he up to? Only the odd Taliban would venture into these parts.

Suddenly I felt the irresistible impulse of pulling the earphones out of my mini-Disc Walkman, clinging them on the kid, and pushing Play. *Baba O'Riley* exploded in his brain. He was transfixed. Long after the intro, all the way to when Roger Daltrey screams *Teenage Wasteland!* at the top of his lungs. *I don't need to fight, to prove I'm right.* Well, I just wanted to prove, maybe, that the power of music could subvert any teenage wasteland—with unforeseen consequences. As we left his slim frame stood there, motionless, gazing at the vanishing jeep in the desert. And that's how The Who Christianized a mini-Taliban.

It happened in a sub-branch of the Silk Road. For years I had been piecing together stretch upon stretch of the Silk Road in my travels across Asia. Until one day it hit me: most of the time I had been following a pilgrim monk. That's his story. It reads like a dream.

Let's go back to the seventh century. Europe was wallowing in medievalism, twilight of civilization-style, while in parallel India and China were consumed by a political, intellectual, religious and artistic vortex, linked by Buddhism, which had managed to create a vast electric current of humanism.

After no less than a thousand years of meditation, Buddhist mysticism had reached unreachable landscapes of the soul. And that happened in parallel to one millennium of Greek-Roman classicism. Humanity, periodically, through myriad attempts, always re-creates itself, lives up to the highest standard of its *raison d'être*, enjoying an usually short and singular apex, just to unravel and be mired all over again in a very slow dissolution.

But let our movie begin, as a swooping camera movement will plunge you right into China's imperial capital Ch'ang-an—the Rome of the East.

Our hero, the young Xuanzang, is a fervent Buddhist heir to a long line of men of letters and mandarins forged into the careful observation of Confucian wisdom and millenary rules of etiquette— what we can describe as the inherent politeness of the Chinese heart.

The empire was plunging into anarchy. So Xuanzang and his brother decide to exile themselves in the mountains of Sichuan. When he's twenty he receives in Chengdu the complement of his monastic rules. The civil war was ending and the Tang were winning. Xuanzang finally makes it to Ch'ang-an.

For five centuries already missionaries coming from India and Kashgaria—what is today Western China—had established monasteries and incessantly translated, from Sanskrit to Chinese, the huge literature of the two Buddhist vehicles, the Hinayana and the Mahayana.

Xuanzang requests from emperor Taizong an authorization to leave China. An imperial decree means a refusal. Taizong, new on the throne, is worried about Chinese subjects leaving towards the unknown. But then one day Xuanzang has a dream. On a night in the year 629 he sees the sacred mountain Sumeru rising from the middle of the ocean. He yearns to reach the summit and plunges into the waves. At this very moment a magic lotus appears under him and deposes him, effortlessly, at the foot of the mountain. But the mountain is huge, and it is impossible to attempt a climbing. Yet a mysterious swirling force places him at the top of the mountain. He faces a limitless horizon and, predictably, is inundated with joy. He awakes. A few days later, Xuanzang leaves for the Great West.

I followed the detailed itinerary of Xuanzang in Western China and Central Asia through the atlases printed in the tome IV of one of ace explorer Aurel Stein's books, *Innermost Asia*. I had taken it with me in my travels but then I lost it—with many other books—in a fire in Thailand. One more lesson learned out of Buddhist impermanence.

Xuanzang was a Confucianist. This meant he exhibited the classic Chinese formal qualities; hereditary politeness and a firm observance of discipline. But he also embodied profound virtues; common sense; circumspection; sense of measure; discretion in everyday life; an infinite *delicatesse* in his friendships; and equanimity.

Thorough the deserts of Gansu he took the road followed by the caravans to Mongolia and the Tarim basin. He crossed markets frequented by all the peoples of the Great West, from the Yellow River to the Pamir mountains. We can see this fabulous crowd in the frescoes of Bazaklik, near Turfan—caravan dwellers from Soghdiana and Turkestan who look, appropriately, Turkish and Iranian.

China ended in Gansu—and the Great West started; steppe upon steppe, and the mysterious sands of the Gobi. Talk about a millenary Chinese dread when facing these enemy solitudes. Further on down the road one would have to face the snowy peaks of the Tian Shan and the Pamir. Frontiers were closed; you needed an imperial authorization to proceed. So Xuanzang kept rolling in secret, hiding during the day, walking by night. He ended up penetrating the desert sands, the unlimited Gobi, the caravan-killer, by himself. Over and over he thought he was facing the armies of Mara—the Buddhist demon. These were, of course, desert mirages.

He got deeper into the Gachun Gobi—which the Chinese call the river of sands. For guidance, he observed, always walking, the direction of his shadow; and he recited the *Prajna Paramita*—Buddhist wisdom—like a mantra. So picture a lonely pilgrim in an infinite desert, facing danger after danger, all the way to India to research some texts and confront metaphysical systems, only guided by his shadow, the mystical flame of a text protecting him from the flames of the sun.

Xuanzang for his trip wanted no riches, no praise, no lasting reputation. His unique aim was to find what he framed as the Superior Intelligence and the Righteous Law.

The Kingdom of Turfan in the seventh century was a key civilization in Central Asia—influenced by both China and Persia. Today it's all gone. The political, economic and cultural life was amazing, as we see in frescoes brought by German explorer von Le Coq to Berlin. Le Coq called the Gandhara Buddhas he found the last "late antiques"— late up to the Middle Ages in Europe, and then forgotten for centuries in time and space deep into the Gobi.

Xuanzang crossed the Tian Shan mountains all the way to the Syr-Darya basin, covered by glaciers which this predecessor of the great nineteenth century explorers like Aurel Stein and Sven Hedin describes as dangerous "mountains of ice" with "summits reaching the heavens." He descended the Tian Shan towards pristine lake Issyk kul—the "hot lake," because it never freezes over. He met the Great Khan of the Western Turks, Tong Yabghu Qaghan, whose empire was at its apex, dominating everywhere from the Altai to the Oxus river and Badakhshan.

Picture a nomad sovereign with a domain whose borders touched Persia and the Chinese empire. The *Tang Annals* describe him as no less than awesome. To better monitor Iran, he established his capital in Tchash, the current Tashkent. On the northeast, the king of Turfan was practically a vassal. To the south, one of his sons was reigning in Bactria. The *History of the Tang* says he held the hegemony over the lineaments of the West. "Never the Barbarians of the West have been so powerful."

His secret was a nomad cavalry. History on horseback. Just like centuries later Hegel would describe Napoleon as the *zeitgeist*—the spirit of the times—on horseback.

So picture a wild, pristine region around lake Issyk kul under the shade of the Tian Shan which overlooks the Chinese world and the Iranian world. History itself was at a crucial Asian crossroads in the seventh century. The ascension of the Tang had opened the way to the predominance of Uyghur tribes in lands west of China. The Sassanid empire—a barrier against Turkish expansion—would be eventually overran by Islam. In Muslim Persia a Turk *condottiere* would be in power, in attendance of the coming Turkish Sultan. And beyond Persia, Byzantium—or Rum—would be finally conquered by Islam in 1453.

Xuanzang kept rolling all the way to Samarkand, traversing the eastern border of the Desert of Red Sands, the Kizil Kum, which separates the Syr-Darya from the Amur-Darya. Samarkand—which the

Chinese called Kang, the name of all Soghdiana—was a very ancient city; Marakanda, already known nine centuries before by Alexander the Great. Marakanda was a watchtower of Persian culture speaking an east Iranian dialect, the soghdian—recreated by the nineteenth century expedition of Paul Pellliot—that caravans from Samarkand had unfurled throughout the Gobi up to Dunhuang in China.

So culture in Transoxiana was oriented towards Persia. Religion was Mazdeism—straight from Zoroaster. But the Soghdians, the caravaners of Central Asia, were also in day-to-day contact with Buddhism.

Xuanzang kept walking—all the way to the Kotin Koh chain, attached to the Pamirs. He reached the Iron Doors—the passage traversed by all caravans between Samarkand and the Oxus, the southern frontier of the empire of the Western Turks. Turks controlled all the traffic between Central Asia and India. South of the Iron Doors, Xuanzang crossed the Oxus—the current Amur-Darya—and entered ancient Bactria, old Iranian land from the dawn of time, which later became a Greek land when conquered by Alexander the Great.

He was seeing for the first time how Greco-Buddhist civilization sprang up—the union of Buddhism and Alexandrine art. He got to Balkh—the ancient Bactria, also heavily Iranian but ardently Buddhist. Today what's left are a few ruined stupas; the Mongol and Muslim devastation spared absolutely no sculptures. After Balkh, Xuanzang did nothing less than cross the Hindu Kush, the "Snowy

Mountains." Through some serious mountain passes he arrived in Bamiyan, a key relay station on the road from Central Asia to India. When Xuanzang was there, Bamiyan had a dozen Buddhist monasteries with thousands of monks. He visited caves incrusted on the mountain—monastic cells. And he talks about the two giant Buddhas—53 meters and 35 meters—which the Taliban would destroy in 2001. I was always fascinated at how a pilgrim monk from China reacted face to face with the last works of the art of Gandhara, a supreme vestige of Hellenism. The Great Buddha was in fact a giant version of a Greek statue. And there were also frescoes—like a Central Asian version of Pompey.

Then it's the Kabul valley, which at the time was already India. He met his first Hindu ascetics, some totally naked, or "dressed in blue" afraid of losing, by possessing a garment, their vow of poverty. Others were Shivaists, the body enveloped in ashes and sporting a hat decorated with skulls. He left the Panjshir all the way to Jalalabad, the ancient city of Nagarahara, with its big stupa built by the Indian emperor Ashoka. That was the site of one of the most venerable legends of Buddhism. In a previous cosmic cycle, a young man—the one that, in his latest incarnation, would become the Buddha Sakyamuni—met the Buddha of these times, Dipankara. And Dipankara predicted to his worshipper his future accession to Buddhahood.

Precious objects a French archeological mission found in the city of Hadda are today exposed at the Guimet museum in Paris; when you see them, you will see what a Greco-Buddhist art nouveau is all about. The magic worked deep into Afghanistan—as the Hellenist schools of Gandhara art went an artistic step ahead. From Greco-Roman art in Kabul and the Punjab, and as a sister of Roman-Syrian art and art from Palmyra, came a completely different version of Gothic-Buddhism. But then the Arabs irrupted in the mid-seventeenth century armed with pious vandalism. If Islam had not intervened, we would have reached unparalleled artistic heights. This—magic—passage from Greco-Roman to Gothic was discovered in Afghanistan no less than nine centuries before Europe.

Xuanzang visited the cavern where the Buddha, after having mastered the *naga*—or dragon king Gopala—left the trace of his shadow. He entered the grotto all alone, and followed the instructions of an old man he met on the road. Fifty steps; touch the eastern border; step back; and stand still. One hundred salutations. Nothing happened. Despair. But then Xuanzang saw a light in the oriental wall. He kept performing the salutations until the whole grotto was inundated by light, white blinding light, revealing the image of the so-called "mountain of gold." The body of the Buddha and his monastic robe was yellowish red; from his face to the knees all was glowing; and downwards his lotus throne was enveloped in a sort of sunset.

It always comes back to Gandhara—which, once again, was already known by the Macedonians. This is where Greek kings, after being expelled from Bactria, went to exile for yet another century. All those Gandhara Buddhas—Apollonian purity profiles with undulating hair and impeccable drapery. So imagine once again waves of Chinese pilgrims after Xuanzang facing the first human images of the Buddha. Two centuries before Xuanzang, Gandhara harbored two of the most important philosophers of Mahayana Buddhism: Asanga and Vasubandhu. Both came from Peshawar—which would, centuries later, under Islam, become the Muslim Rome, the Rome of the East, and where I learned from wise men over endless cups of green tea all there is to know about that post-modern myth called al-Qaeda, before a sci-fi operation dubbed 9/11 was devised, designed, financed, produced, stage-managed, directed and sold by an emaciated Arab with disintegrating kidneys straight out of a cave in Silk Road Afghanistan "because he hated our freedoms." But that's another story. When Xuanzang hit Peshawar, it was one century after the Hun invasion which would destroy Ghandaran civilization.

Xuanzang went deeper into India, crossing the Indus and entering Punjab, and the great city of Taxila. Centuries later, the Indian Archeological Service would identify, under the modern Saraikala site, at least three juxtaposed cities: the ancient city of king Taxila; the Greek city of the ruler Eukratides; and a third one maybe founded by the Indo-Scythian emperor Kanishka.

Then Kashmir—and its intense religious life. In the fourth century Kashmir harbored one of the top philosophical schools of Shivaism. When Xuanzang was there Buddhism was still spread out among a hundred monasteries housing 5,000 monks—amidst three stupas built by Indian emperor Ashoka, and memories from Kanishka; these were like the Constantine and the Clovis of Buddhism. The King of Kashmir came to meet Xuanzang in person on a road inundated with flowers and perfume. He allocated twenty scribes at Xuanzang's beck and call to find copies of sutras as well as philosophical treaties. Xuanzang spent two years in Kashmir until he descended from the high valleys towards the sacred land of the Ganges to find traces of the Buddha.

He met Brahmins who were extremely versed on the Madhyami-ka, Buddhist criticism so radical that the West couldn't do better than label it as nihilism. Madhyamika is the Middle Way, founded in Dekhan, around the first century, by philosopher Nagarjuna. It's a system built around a particularly subtle dialectic, really hardcore, only understood in the West by counter-sense, as is so difficult to render Indian concepts with a Western equivalent. Thus a "nihilist" doctrine, a theory of the Void and of Nothing. And yet *sunyata* does not exactly correspond to "void." I only understood it many years after I first retraced the Buddha's steps in India. Madhyamika is Buddhist metaphysics—no less than seventeen centuries before Kant. It was a sort of critique of pure reason. And in a theory of the world as will and representation, *sunyata* shines as a state of mind and spir-it liberated from representation and from will. No wonder we in the West could not possibly grasp it.

And this is how we see the many degrees of separation between the Indian and the Western spirit. An absolute simplification leading to vacuity, under Western logic, equals nihilism. The Indian, on the other hand, as he sees himself intellectually and morally free of all attachment, purified in his spirit as well as in his senses, finds in this liberation of all the data of what we call "reality," in this deliverance, the source of an immense mystical joy, the cause of an amazing *élan vital*.

If we plunge deep down in our Ego we must have it dissolved. In place of this world of moral pain and material obstacles, an abyss without apparent end enthralls the heart. It's like a luminous, submarine abyss, impermeable but also full of ineffable beauty, fleeting profoundness and infinite transparencies. At the surface of this vacuity, the mirage of things plays with changing colors. They are not what they seem. As we plunge into intimate contemplation of this endless profoundness, depth, matchless purity of the absolute vacuity, the mirage dissipates. All virtualities appear, all powers are activated. We go beyond the looking glass.

Xuanzang found libraries crammed with essential texts as well as doctors versed on all philosophical secrets of the Great Way in the ancient land of Kurukshetra—an isthmus between the Indus basin to the west and the Ganges to the east, between the Himalayas to the north and the desert of Rajputana to the south. In legendary times, this is where the *Mahabharata* happened, the shock of the Kaurava and the Pandava for hegemony over the Ganges. Xuanzang could hear Krishna saying, *Life and death are like an ocean without borders and flow in an endless alternance.*

He finally reached Kapilavastu, where the Buddha was born, once home to thousands of monasteries whose ruins he could see everywhere in the middle of the jungle. The site was only identified in the early twentieth century because of a pillar inscribed by emperor Ashoka found in Lumpini, the garden where the Buddha was born, at the doors of Kapilavastu. And Xuanzang could see where, gone with his chariot to the countryside, the young prince first saw Old Age, Sickness and Death, the symbolic encounter that would forge his life.

The Lumpini garden is where Queen Maya, standing up, holding with her right hand the branch of a tree, gave birth to the prince. The divine child left from her right flank, received by the arms of Indra and Brahma, the supreme god of Vedism and the supreme god of Brahmanism. The baby took possession of the world by walking seven steps in each of the fourth directions. A pillar was in the middle of the garden, and that was what identified Lumpini.

Xuanzang also saw the landscape in which the Buddha entered nirvana. On the margins of river Hiranyavati, the Buddha prepared himself a bed between two trees which were soon covered by flowers. He consoled his disciple Ananda. *How is it possible that what was born, subject to instability, does not pass away?* And he re-stressed that everything that is created is perishable.

Xuanzang then went to Benares—which even inhabited mostly by Hinduists, had not forgotten the Buddha. In Sarnath, he dwelled through the Antelope Park, the site of the first predication of the Buddha, or the setting in movement of the Wheel of the Law. That was the site of the Benares Sermon—where the Buddha laid out the rejection of a life of extremes, and delineated the Middle Way, which leads to peace, science, illumination and nirvana. If everything is pain, suppression of pain must be achieved by suppressing desire. The Middle Way. Your way towards the sun, which is inbuilt in your name: Ayan.

Xuanzang went further to Bodhgaya—the heart of Buddhism, the sacred site where the Buddha, under a tree, was illuminated and obtained Wisdom. He could easily visualize the motionless *boddhisattva*, under the tree, concentrating his thought on universal pain and how to abolish it.

Then there was all the arduous way back. Xuanzang stopped at Dunhuang—an apotheosis of Buddhist caves—waiting for his supplication to king Taizong to be granted a favorable response. It was in Dunhuang that the voyagers from the Great West could finally rest. A prime Buddhist center—and we know that because of the frescoes and paintings on silk banners brought back to the Guimet museum in Paris by Pelliot and to the British Museum by Aurel Stein, originally at the Grotto of a Thousand Buddhas. Side by side with a *bodhisattva*'s naked torso, enveloped in transparent Indian scarves, we would find another one, fully Sinicized. In this key crossroads of the history of Chinese thinking and culture, in a place crossed by all the caravans coming from India and Iran, many centuries later we would finally understand how Tang China received, interpreted and adapted countless influences from abroad.

It had been ten years after an obscure monk first went beyond the pale and traversed the Gobi, the Tian Shan, the Hindu Kush, the Indus, the Ganges, the Pamirs. Would the Chinese court react with a very predictable foul mood? Instead, Xuanzang was welcomed as a hero. Fabulous entrance in Ch'ang-an, through the Street of the Red Bird, then solemnly transported to the monastery of Big Happiness with all the relics, statues and manuscripts he brought from India. He would translate 600 manuscripts from Sanskrit helped by a team of translators, silently creating correct equivalents to the extremely delicate terminology of Indian metaphysics. When the first collection was finished, in the autumn of 648, emperor Taizong wrote a preface in a calligraphy "precious like silver and jade" and bound to last "as long as heaven and earth." And Xuanzang of course handed to the king the travel book of his whole extraordinary adventure.

玄奘

I see Xuanzang as a mix between Pausanias—his equivalent in the Greek world—and a post-modern reporter. He led me to the myriad Silk Roads across Central and South Asia as much as Conrad led me to Southeast Asia. Now you know.

I could dream you, Dad and me crossing the Northwest Passage, conquered just over a century ago—as we would feel overwhelmed by all that ice erosion. Dad would have taught you how ice reflects radiation. No ice, and what is revealed below are the Arctic's dark, dark waters. Constantly, less and less solar radiation is being reflected back into space as the Arctic warms up. Remove sea ice as the foundation for life and you get what your generation will inherit, a mighty colossal and alarmingly dangerous… "experiment."

But before crossing the Northwest Passage, the dream would be for our triad to follow the Silk Roads. That's what I would be doing anyway—from before you being born to Big Sleep day. By then you would have read some of what your Funky Grandpa wrote, after all it's all over the surveilled, monopolized, sanitized by common sense, copyright, control and conformism net where, in theory, remains indestructible. And that means I won't bother you with politics.

Waaall, as Pound would say, perhaps just a bit. All you need to know, from Sun Tzu and Machiavelli to Alice in Wonderland, is who's in power. How. Why. For what purpose. And why do we have wars. Because as much as now—as you're being born—as in now, when you read this letter, we are ruled by an overlapping elite of psychopaths who own the financial system and control governments and media. Their modus operandi is to fund both sides of war for profit and manufacture public consent through media propaganda.

You are a EU citizen—sorry, a citizen in an endlessly fragmented collection of nation-states collectively referred to as "Europe." I'm not partial to crystal balls. No one predicted the fall of the Soviet Union as it happened. The Cold War—under which my generation grew up—was a hell freezes over op. The old Soviet Union was contained from the North Cape—around Norway—to Pakistan. As you're born, Cold War 2.0 is installing a virtual wall from the Baltic Sea to the Black Sea.

What is certain is that you are being born in a EU where Germany is an economic colossus with clay feet, incapable of a truly visionary pan-European project. You are being born into a EU where fathers and mothers despair about their unemployed—or underpaid—sons and daughters; their slashed pensions; their neglected public services. You are being born right into the most serious economic crisis since the Depression in the 1930s—possibly the early warning sign of an endless stagnation. You will be hurled smack into the eye of the hurricane, as a member of the first generation to emerge into something completely different; the closing of a historical phase that lasted half a millennium—the rule of the White Man over the whole planet, starting with the "Great" Discoveries and throughout colonialism. It's as if History's pendulum—the Angel of History's vengeance?—would be sending us back half a millennium ago, when Chindia was the center of the world, wealthier, more populous, more advanced.

Before I slip into the Big Sleep, what we know, Little Techno Guy, is that we are in a—Gramsci—flicker; when the Old Order is slowly dying and the New Order has not been born yet. It may be Pax Eurasia. Or it may be all-out war. And this while the next technological revolution—robotics, genetic engineering, artificial intelligence—will render so much human activity completely irrelevant.

So now it's your time to hit the road—and start making your mark. You've got a little help from those friends—from Conrad to Rimbaud to the beats. You know Desolation Row could be anywhere—corruption drenched on corruption like in a film noir. Desolation of the soul, misery of humanity, a post-everything ultra-regressive neoliberal status quo mirrored in a parallel dimension, peopled by dodgy characters, visions and allusions. Some desperate, desolate mindscape, crammed with zombie prisoners, that looks like the projection of a dream turning into nightmare.

So you will deploy your own *machine de guerre*—a remix of those old friends Deleuze and Guattari in the *Anti-Oedipus*. Use as RPGs everything that I could bring to you as a gift—a life of fragments. Pre-Socratics. Baudelaire. Benjamin. Baudrillard. Cioran. Borges— the Buddha in a grey suit. Eliot. *These fragments I have shored against my ruins.* Every fragment envelops a world in itself and thus a— fragmented—truth. Which may contradict the following truth, and thus to infinity.

Perhaps you will find, quite early, that we can do little else than parade some sort of chic spleen embellished by Greek sophistry.

Skepticism—the elegance of anxiety—is such a balsam. You may also identify as nonsense that constant demeaning of Buddhism depicted as "just" another form of skepticism. Nonsense. Thus you may instead lean towards some semi-divinities of Chinese mythology like the Ho-Ho—installed midway between heaven and earth spending their time roaring with laughter telling themselves the latest human imbecilities.

You will have learned from Tibetan Buddhism that the world exists— but it's not real. The Buddha picks up a lotus flower and smiles. What does it mean? What matters is the smile itself. The meaning of desire, of disgust, of serenity? The meaning of nirvana? For the Buddha, that's all soooo excessive. No possible answer.

And what if it is all just a dream in the end? Borges tells us how a Mongol emperor in the thirteenth century—Kublai Khan—dreamed a palace and had it built according to his vision; in the eighteenth century, an English poet—Coleridge—who could not possibly know that this construction was born in a dream, dreams a poem about the palace. So you will wonder about the symmetry operating on the soul of Men encompassing continents and centuries. *We live as we dream. Alone.* But also in selected company.

Riverrun—as Joyce in *Finnegans Wake*—and you will keep coming back to the same river. Everything flows. And then, one fine day, in a flicker, trespassed by an illumination, you will see that you have crossed to the other side. The *sunyata* effect. The West into which you're being born could only conceive "nothingness"—a sordid version of the void, to explain *sunyata*. Yet the void is the metaphysical dimension of silence. The void is the extreme nuance of silence.

The dahlias sleep in the empty silence. Dear Ayan. Enjoy the silence.